GREAT CITIES OF THE WORLD — HONG KONG

Colonial merchant houses and untouched hills of 19th century Hong Kong in this example of the Chinese school of painting

GREAT CITIES OF THE WORLD

HONG KONG

Published by Formasia
Written by Ian Buruma
Photographed by Frank Fischbeck
Designed by Robert Hookham
Produced by Format Limited
© Formasia Ltd. All rights reserved
First Edition 1987
Second Edition February 1988
ISBN 962-7283-02-9
Printed in Hong Kong by
Paramount Printing Company Limited

Hong Kong is one of the world's great monuments to human endeavour

HONG KONG is a bit like a fat man with too much gold in his mouth. It is easy to feel contemptuous of the place, which many regard as little more than a huge shopping arcade with an airport. The dollar could be Hong Kong's official emblem; The Wealth of Nations its bible and the Hang Seng index its health chart.

Making money is of course the business of every modern city...well, perhaps not of Pyongyang, but it is certainly the business of every capitalist city. Hong Kong is the consummate capitalist city, based on interest, in every sense of the word, from bank rates to free information. Pyongyang and other communist, or, indeed, religious capitals, like Tehran, are not based on interest, but on ideas: the worker's paradise, the glorious egalitarian millenium and so forth. So far, interest, or greed, if you prefer to be blunt, has been kinder to people than ideas. The banker, after all, has a stake in our prosperity; the commissar or the mullah care less: their interest is in our soul, not our wallet, a crucial difference.

But the materialist ethos of Hong Kong is so overwhelming that one feels a little uneasy about it nonetheless; especially if one has been raised in the soft socialism of postwar Europe. Milton Friedman thinks Hong Kong is wonderful, which really says enough.

But before condemning Hong Kong for its crassness, let us consider why Hong Kong is what it is. Hong Kong has, it seems to me, always been inspired by two things: greed and deprivation. The two merge into one another of course; deprivation can result in greed. It is a characteristic already apparent as the visitor arrives in Kai Tak airport. His hands still clammy after the experience of seeing the wing tips of his plane almost smashing the windows of highrise buildings on the final approach to the airport, the visitor will want to change some money into the local currency, the Hong Kong dollar. Only after he leaves Kai Tak will he realize that he has got considerably less for his money than at any bank down town. It is a most fitting welcome to Hong Kong, an early warning to be on one's toes in the city of interest. Just beware of the instant friend who has a special bargain "only for you, my friend." The ethics of Hong Kong are the ethics of the bazaar. The exorbitant exchange rates of Kai Tak not withstanding, the Hong Kong bazaar can often be surprisingly honest. But don't expect anybody to shed tears for the sucker.

Big bucks have their own aesthetics. In Hong Kong, like in New York, Chicago or the City of London, wealth is expressed in Big Bang corporate architecture. Corporate status is measured in bricks or glass, preferably golden glass. Hong Kong's Central District is filled with tributes to the power of Chinese entrepreneurs and British bankers. The most spectacular building is the new headquarters of the Hong Kong and Shanghai bank, or, as its employees like to say, in their plummy voices, the Hongkers and Shankers. It is said to be the most expensive buidling in the world. The style is that of the Beaubourg Centre in Paris; it wears its insides out. Some find it hideous; others, including myself, love it. Nobody can be indifferent to it. Bruce Chatwin, the great British writer, compared it to a British battleship in the China Sea. It does look like a high-tech destoyer, pulled upright by some miracle of engineering.

The Communist Chinese, not to be outdone by the running dogs of capitalism, have added some buildings of their own on the waterfront, notably the uninspiring China Resources building. But soon the China Bank building should be completed. It is, naturally, going to be even higher than the Hongkers and Shankers. What does this mean? That the Chinese are prepared to spend a fortune for national pride, in other words, for an idea? Or, that the Chinese take their bank very seriously, which means interest? The future of Hong Kong depends on the answer.

The greed of the 19th century opium traders who founded Hong Kong was of a peculiar kind. Most of them were upright Scotsmen who firmly believed that accumulating wealth was a moral thing to do. The rich man was obviously favoured by God, for otherwise, why would he be rich? These Scottish pioneers were, after all, good Protestants. The Chinese, educated in Confucian ethics, understood this Western morality perfectly well. To them, too, getting rich was a noble end in itself. Wealth is good for the family, and what is good for the Chinese family is by definition virtuous. Even if the wealth has not been acquired by the most scrupulous of means, by outright gangsterism, let us say, such sins can be overlooked if enough of the wealth finds its way into virtuous charities, schools, libraries and the like. It has become rather popular these days for Hong Kong millionaires to cleanse their greedy souls (as well as buying future good will) by sending money to China, the poor old motherland, which needs cash like a desert needs rain.

The sober Scots and ambitious Cantonese share a deep conviction that we are on earth to work, not to play. People do play in Hongkong, though, but in a somewhat grim, businesslike manner. Sex, sports, or any other kind of recreation, usually boils down to the pursuit Hong Kong knows best: making money. Take the bargirls, whose presence in East Asia one can hardly overlook: Thais and Filipinas pretend to have a good time, and sometimes maybe they do, while the eyes of Wanchai girls only light up when the shallow banter turns to more substantial matters, like paying the bill. This attitude suits the Cantonese, and possibly those dour Scotsmen too. Fun becomes less sinful if making money is the purpose. The other great Hong Kong recreation besides the stockmarket, is horse-racing. There is one track in the middle of Hong Kong Island, and one out in the New Territories. Foreign dignitaries go to the races to pretend they are at Ascot — floppy hats and champers — the Chinese go to make money of course.

The only people who appear to be having a really carefree good time in Hong Kong are the new breed of white expatriates, or in local parlance "expats." You see them on Sundays, on their boats: beefy young Australians with rugby football thighs, filling themselves with beer; red-faced Englishmen and healthy Americans in jokey T-shirts who divide their time between working out in gyms and making fortunes. These are the new incarnations of the planters, traders and civil servants that used to come East to make good. Their only anxiety is that one day they will be sent back to Darwin, Croydon or Hoboken.

To many Chinese Hong Kong represented hope. Like San Francisco, it was the Golden Mountain. Hong Kong is, in a way, the base camp of a worldwide range of golden mountains — the capital, in short, of China-town. China for many centuries squeezed its unhappiest citizens out to richer pastures. There have been many times in China, when for countless people it became simply intolerable to live there. The reasons for these turbulent times could be brutal rulers, war or famine, or sometimes a combination of all three. The dream of distant mountains were the traditional safety valve. And it was not always very safe. The ghastly slave trade from Africa is well known. Less often written about is the treatment of Chinese coolies, stuffed into stinking vessels bound for Malaya, Cuba or Peru. About half of them died on the way, suffocated by the crush, or starved and crazy with thirst. Still, some actually made it up that golden mountain. In Hong Kong, more than some. It says something about our times that for the first time in history the safety valve of Hong Kong has been turned off.

Hong Kong is full. The Chinatown of refugees can no longer offer a haven. It is a melancholy sight: the peasants from Canton, attracted by Chinatown's bright lights and the promise of freedom to pursue gold, hunted down at border fences by police dogs, and turned back to the rigours of the People's Republic. Even more melancholy is the sight of mothers and children being sent back, after having joined their husbands, who dashed to Hong Kong first. But most melancholy of all are the Vietnamese, often refugees from the Chinatowns of Indochina. There they are, often for years, some maybe even forever, huddled in the closed camps, dreaming of a future outside the barbed wire, if not for themselves, at least for their children. If some Hong Kong people appear a little callous about the fate of these unfortunates, it is not because they do not understand their plight. It is, rather, because they do, only too well. But for the grace of God,... They are too busy looking after themselves to worry much about others. Safety, wealth, success, these are all precarious matters.

Fortunes are lost as quickly as they are won in Hong Kong. Stockmarkets are a bit like casinos everywhere, but nowhere more so than in Hong Kong. It either shoots up, like a high-stake poker game in Vegas, or it comes tumbling down. It is not a gentlemen's game, but one for gamblers, and Hong Kong is, partly by necessity, partly perhaps by inclination, a city of born gamblers. Every day in Hong Kong is like a day at the races: people from all classes and walks of life crowd around TV monitors at street corners to gaze at the latest stockmarket figures, calculating how much has been lost or won.

Black Monday of 1987 prompted jokes in London and New York about $200,000 a year Yuppies losing their Porsches. Such people lost their silk shirts in Hong Kong too. But more typical of this gambling city was the fate of the old lady who cleans the office I work in. She can hardly write her name, has spent a lifetime mopping floors, but was also an inveterate investor in stocks. All her savings went into the Great Casino, possibly in the hope of making enough to send her sons to universities abroad, in America or Australia, thereby securing residents' permits and green cards, those ultimate tickets to freedom. She lost everything. For about two days she mopped the office floor, muttering to herself, as if in a state of shock. Then, suddenly, she recovered completely and shrugged the experience off like a hardened gambler. You win some, you lose some; another day, another dollar. Our cleaning lady, much more than the governor in his white gala uniform, could serve as the symbol of Hong Kong, its weakness and its strength.

When I am in a European soft-socialist mood, I think of an interview I once read with Joseph Brodsky, the famous Russian poet, who won the Nobel Prize for literature in 1987. He was just exiled from the Soviet Union. His interviewer asked him whether he found the displays of abundance in Western shops morally disturbing. Brodsky was baffled by the question. He then launched a tirade against the dismal material conditions of Soviet life. I was reminded of this story again quite recently, when a Chinese acquaintance arrived in Hong Kong from Peking on her first trip abroad. She was speechless with pleasure when she saw the wealth of fruit and vegetables available at the local supermarket.

Deprivation, to be sure, can make a fetish out of wealth, or even security. The fetish for food, though a common Chinese trait, must be due to this. Like Jewish mammas with their roots in medieval ghettos, Chinese mothers love to see their families eat; the more the better. Like the French, the other nation of food fetishists, the Cantonese will eat almost anything. The more fastidious northern Chinese find this somewhat barbaric, a bit like the puritanical British looking down their noses at the French for eating frogs. The Cantonese eat anything, the northerners like to say, that swims or flies, as long as it is not made of metal. The only reason such delicacies as owl, eagle or chow dog are not eaten in Hong Kong, at least not openly, is because the fastidious British forbid it.

Hong Kong, the city born of greed and deprivation, is perhaps most truly itself, more so even than at the stock exchange, the jewelry shops or the street markets, in that most archetypal of Hong Kong institutions: the dim sum palace. The dim sum palaces are to Hong Kong what railway stations were to Victorian England, skyscrapers to 20th century America, pagodas to Burma or churches to Rome — they express the highest aspirations of a people. They are the cathedrals of food worship. Dim Sum restaurants even have a kind of ecclesiastical hierarchy, as it were, expressed in different uniforms worn for different tasks. There are people to take orders, people to cart the snacks around, others to put the food on the table, and others yet to add up the bill. What people celebrate in the gigantic, gaudy, golden dim sum halls where thousands partake of shrimp dumplings, spring rolls, chicken feet and other delicacies is very real — it is nothing more or less than the blessing of a full stomach.

Hong Kong is a Chinese city. That is to say, it is a Cantonese city. The Cantonese, while regarding themselves as Chinese, are convinced of their superiority over all other Chinese. They think they are smarter and better at making money (perhaps the ultimate Cantonese standard of a man's worth). They like to point out that the Cantonese language, which is unintelligible to a northerner, is closer to the Chinese spoken one thousand years ago, hence superior. And of course they believe that their cuisine, including the owls, cobras, eagles and dogs, is in a different class from the greasy Shanghainese fare or the bread dumplings of Peking.

Still, there are other Chinese in Hong Kong, notably Shanghainese, who fled in 1949, and Chiu Chows, from the northeast of Canton province. The Chiu Chows, or Teo Chews, as they are called in Southeast Asia, are masters of many trades, including Chinese medicine, often with purported aphrodisiac effects — ground rhinoceros horn, dried bull's penis, and the like. Given their strong clan connections in Bangkok, a Chew Chow city, Chiu Chow gangsters do a good business in harder drugs too.

Altogether, the Chiu Chows, Cantonese, Shanghainese, Hokkienese, and other Chinese form 98% of the people living in Hong Kong. The rest are Filipinos, Indians, Taiwanese, Japanese and assorted foreign devils. There are more Americans — about 14000 — than British living in this last major British colony. Hong Kong is Chinese, but not yet part of China. Or, more accurately, it is not yet part of the Chinese state. There are basically two Chinas: the state and the civilization. Hong Kong belongs to the latter. The paradox is that the gap between the state and the civilization as lived by overseas Chinese has widened in the last fifty years. Chinatowns, from Bangkok to Vancouver, from Amsterdam to Hong Kong, have become richer and richer in rather similar ways to the mercantile Scots who built Hong Kong a century ago; what the West pushed on China then, is being paid back with interest today.

Chinatown Chinese are both more modern and more traditional than the Chinese of China. They have clung to traditions, customs and superstitions that the Maoists tried, with varying success, to wipe out in the People's Republic. Open a Hong Kong newspaper and you will see the most sophisticated analysis of world economic trends, or a perceptive critique of a Mozart opera. You will also find articles about ritual murders in the criminal underworld; or an item about men who cut the whiskers off a seal, hoping that by eating them they would be assured of virility and longevity. Hong Kong appears to be able to live with these contrasts without much trouble. Whatever other problems it may have, the city is comfortable with the modern world — a world based on materialism, individual enterprise and free information. Hong Kong, though, as I said, Chinese, has outgrown China. Yet soon it is to be grafted back onto the motherland; state and civilization are to be sewn together again. This promises to be a painful operation.

One can see some of the stitches already. The number of people who can speak Mandarin, the standard language of China, is growing. So is the number of TV programmes, magazine articles, books and films about "mainland" culture. How much criticism of modern China, whether in the form of Taiwanese films or local journalism, to allow is a highly sensitive issue. Criticism of China worries the last British colonial rulers for two reasons: it might upset the future communist masters, and it might panic their future subjects.

The power already wielded by representatives of the People's Republic can be seen almost nightly on TV. Whenever a Chinese politician, these days usually a smiling figure in a Western suit, appears at a conference, he is surrounded by a mob of Hong Kong reporters trying to catch his every pearl of wisdom in their microphones, held up like loving cups.

Hong Kong's success is not hard to explain. It is an international city perched on the back of a huge communist empire. Hong Kong's international status means free trade and information, financial expertise and experience in dealing with foreigners. This is the image Hong Kong wishes to project. This is why the present governer, Sir David Wilson, is pleased to hear the Japanese Consul-General calling Hong Kong "the most important international metropolis in Asia", and why he quotes the US Consul General as saying that Hong Kong shares such values as individual rights and freedoms with the West. Maybe. It will be interesting to see just how international Hong Kong will remain in the future, without British rule. Even now, fewer people in Hong Kong speak English than Singaporeans, who live in the other financial centre of the region. To what extent future generations should be educated as English-speaking cosmopolitans, sophisticated but unsure of their cultural roots, and to what extent as Chinese, is a matter of crucial concern.

Chinatown culture, like every culture, is based on shared myths. The shared popular myths of Hong Kong culture, often expressed in Cantonese, laced with English, are linked to the mother country; indeed, they are in some respects a caricature of it. Just as British colonial culture is often a caricature of English life. The city slickers in Central working for Jardines or "The Bank," in their pinstripes and club ties, look stagey; their accents are a little too plummy, their wives' chatter about "the servants problem" a little too shrill, and the surnames a little too double-barrelled.

The popular Hong Kong fantasies are exemplified by Kungfu movies. They are about a world that never existed, an exile's dream of life back home. The perfect world of omniscient, invincible spiritual masters and their ever-obedient pupils; of spiritual Chinese ways always winning against the soulless materialism of the West. These myths did not originate in Hong Kong, but in China. They were especially popular when a backward China was first confronted with the far more powerful West. Chinese then did not yearn for a lost mother country, but for a lost, fictional past. The lost Eden that Hong Kong movie audiences and Kungfu comic readers dream of has little to do with China today. Mainland Chinese may dream of Hong Kong, perhaps as a grand house of gilded sin and golden opportunities, but few Hong Kong Chinese ever dream of Peking as a place to live. Even the tenacious Chinese patriotism that many overseas and local Chinese share, and which is shamelessly exploited by Peking, has more to do with the civilization than with the state—the myths are stronger than reality. Reality, however, is what Hong Kong will have to face.

The saddest irony of Hong Kong is that for the first time in history there is a generation of people to whom Hong Kong is truly home. They were not people in transit, dreaming of going back to China, or of golden mounains abroad. They did not escape from anywhere; they were born here, and had no plans to leave. For the first time we find intellectuals and artists, who express themselves as Hong Kongers, not as displaced mainlanders or fake Westerners. Their consciousness has often been shaped by some years of education abroad, in Europe or America. That they chose to come back showed their commitment to Hong Kong. The irony is that their Hong Kong will probably disappear, or change beyond recognition. And these same young people, who returned to Hong Kong, will sooner or later be inclined to leave the place that may no longer seem so much like home.

At least Hongkong knows what it is up against. It is no longer, to use that hackneyed phrase, a borrowed place on borrowed time. There is some security in this. But is security necessarily a good thing? Could it not be that insecurity was one of the main well-springs of Hong Kong's dynamism—as, indeed, it is of dynamic immigrant communities everywhere. You never knew how long Hong Kong was going to last; you had to "make it" fast. This feeling of urgency, this necessity for speed, will last a while longer. It may even be revved up a little, as more people will want to make it and get out before they are overtaken by history. But once the return of China becomes reality, and borrowed time becomes eternal time, the urge to succeed may slacken; fatalism or Oriental wisdom, whatever you wish to call it, may sap the dynamism of Hong Kong. The shopping arcades, the supermarkets, the stock exchange, the banks will still be there, but the phrenetic pace of the city may slow down. The fat man with the gold in his mouth might become an old age pensioner, dozing in the noonday sun. Hong Kong might even become a more pleasant place to live in. But it would not be the Hong Kong we know today; which would be a shame. For the sight of a sinking battleship, never mind how much one deplores its purpose, is a melancholy one.

Ian Buruma

A marriage arranged — and rearranged — by history

18th and early 19th centuries: European merchant trade peacefully at Canton, South China's main city. The West wanted China's teas, silks, and porcelain — the Chinese bought cotton goods, musical clocks and opium from the tall ships from unbelievably far away.

1840: Forbidden by the Chinese authorities to ship opium into the country, Britain sends a powerful fleet to harass China's coastline as far north as Tientsin.

1841: Officers of the Royal Navy land on Hong Kong Island and claim it for the Crown.

1842: British naval force occupies Amoy, Ningpo and Chusan Island. On August 29, while the British are menacing Nanking, a treaty is signed there ceding Hong Kong Island to Britain in perpetuity and opening five ports to trade. China pays an "indemnity" of 21 million silver dollars. A subsequent document, the Treaty of the Bogue (Boca Tigris, at the entrance to the Pearl River) establishes that foreigners should not be subject to Chinese law — the principle of extra-territoriality. Sir Henry Pottinger becomes Governor of Hong Kong.

1843: Treaty of Nanking ratified.

1844: Executive and Legislative Councils set up.

1856: Dispute over a Hong Kong-registered but Chinese-owned small ship, the *Arrow*, escalates into a war in which France joins Britain in attacking Tientsin in retaliation for execution of a French missionary.

1858: British and French capture Tientsin. Treaty of Tientsin signed, giving Britain sovereignty over Kowloon Peninsula and Stonecutter's Island.

1860: Anglo-French force invades Peking and destroys the old Summer Palace. Treaty of Tientsin ratified. The opium trade is legalised and becomes a monopoly of the Hong Kong government, which licences it out.

1895: China defeated in a war with Japan over Korea; the Great Powers seize parcels of territory and concessions, benefiting from China's weakness.

1898: Under the Convention of Peking, Hong Kong is enlarged with a 99-year-lease to Britain of the New Territories and outlying islands, which the British consider necessary for the Colony's defence.

1910: Hong Kong Government officially closes down opium dens.

1925 — 26: Hong Kong's port crippled by a year-long boycott and strike organized by the Chinese Kuomintang (Nationalist Party) headed by Chiang Kai-shek.

1941: Japan attacks Hong Kong on December 1, and captures it on Christmas Day.

1945: British Government re-established in Hong Kong.

1949: Chinese communists defeat the Kuomintang. Mao Tse-tung proclaims: "The Chinese people have stood up." Chiang flees with some of his army to Taiwan.

1950: Korean War breaks out. Hong Kong's manufacturing industry begins a 30-year boom. Population climbs to over 2 million, swollen by refugees from China.

1956: Riots among feuding Kuomintang and communist supporters are quelled by Hong Kong police.

1961 — 62: Huge influx of famine victims from China.

1964: Gulf of Tonkin incident. Vietnam war is enlarged, Hong Kong becomes an important area for supply of US ships, recreation for soldiers and sailors and manufacture of textiles for US market.

1966: Riots over a minute fare increase on the Star Ferry shake Hong Kong. Cultural Revolution begins in China. A dozen leftist rioters are shot dead in Macau.

1967: Labour disputes in Hong Kong quickly lead to communist-inspired riots, denunciations of Britain and Hong Kong Government for "oppression" of Chinese people. British Army is called out to back up the police. Some rioters and policemen are killed. Red Guards burn British Embassy in Peking, but Hong Kong rioters receive no crucial backing from China. Disturbances gradually subside. People's Liberation Army quells some of the unrest in China.

1969: Ninth Party Congress in Peking backs coalition of Maoists and Army led by Defence Minister Lin Biao. Fighting breaks out on Sino-Soviet border.

1971: Lin Biao dies after allegedly plotting to

assassinate Mao. "Ping-pong diplomacy" between China and US begins. China is seated at the United Nations.

1972: President Nixon visits China and signs Shanghai Communique. Britain and Japan normalise diplomatic relations with China. US and China open Liaison Offices in each other's capitals, and trade is resumed.

1973: Arch-pragmatist Deng Xiaoping is rehabilitated in Peking. "Anti-Confucius campaign" begins, with Mao's wife Jiang Qing and other Politburo leftists aiming to overthrow Premier Zhou Enlai.

1974: Independent Commission Against Corruption set up in Hong Kong. Hong Kong Government reaches agreement to reduce flow of legal migrants from China in exchange for bigger effort to catch and send back illegal immigrants.

1975: Leftists' anti-Deng campaign gains strength in China.

1976: Premier Zhou Enlai dies. Hua Guofeng appointed Acting Premier. Anti-leftist riots in Peking are blamed on Deng Xiaoping, who is disgraced a second time. Tangshan earthquake kills some half-million people. Mao dies. Jiang Qing and other members of "Gang of Four" purged and arrested.

1977: Deng rehabilitated again. Hua Guofeng is Chairman and Premier. Hong Kong begins to benefit from new open-door policy in Chinese trade and finance.

1978: Illegal immigration hits a new peak of some 200,000, not counting new flood of seaborne refugees from Vietnam. Deng purges his left-wing enemies in Peking.

1979: Governor Sir Murray MacLehose visits Peking and meets Deng.

1980 — 82: Deng gradually erodes position of Hua Guofeng, ousting him from his top posts.

1982: MacLehose is succeeded as Governor of Hong Kong by Sir Edward Youde, previously British Ambassador in Peking. Vice-Chairman Peng Zhen announces that Hong Kong, Taiwan and Macau will be given "special administrative region" status when reabsorbed into the People's Republic. Mrs Thatcher visits China and Hong Kong, quarrels with Deng over Hong Kong sovereignty issue. Hong Kong Dollar and stockmarket tumble. Negotiations over Hong Kong's future commence in Peking.

1984: China and Britain reach agreement over Hong Kong, which will be permitted to retain it's capitalist system and British laws for 50 years after it reverts to Chinese sovereignty in 1997.

1986: With accustomed pomp and ceremony China invites Queen Elizabeth II to visit Peking the first British monarch ever to do so. The stock market booms. Hong Kong again does what it is best at — earning it's way in a precarious world.

1987: While attending talks in Beijing, on the best way to hand over British sovereignty over Hong Kong to the People's Republic of China, Sir Edward Youde, the quiet, but surprisingly popular 26th Governor, died in his hotel bed.

The Central district of Hong Kong is one of the most expensive bits of real estate in the world; wall to wall corporate power. Above Central, on the Peak is where some of the corporate power-holders live. Between Hong Kong Island and Kowloon lies a harbour full of frenzied activity. Some have swam across it; more people, however, prefer the Star Ferry. Beyond Kowloon lie the New Territories and China

As in New York or Chicago, wealth is expressed in corporate architecture. Hong Kong's Central district is filled with tributes to the power of Chinese entrepreneurs and British banks. The most spectacular building is the new headquarters of the Hongkong and Shanghai Bank, above to the left of the Mandarin Hotel

A relic of the past which has survived the currents of change and the storms of
ideology, and sailed gently from one century into the next: the Chinese junk. It sailed into
Hong Kong harbour long before the supertankers and is still one of the
most spectacular sights of the South China coast. Home in port at Chinese New Year,
thousands of junks are moored side by side in one of many typhoon shelters

It is appropriate that one of the great annual Hong Kong celebrations should take place on the water: the Dragon Boat Festival. In a tradition that is said to go back 2300 years, dragon-shaped boats from all over the Chinese, and these days also non-Chinese world, compete over a 800-yard course, accompanied by drums, cymbals and all the considerable noise that thousands of Cantonese can muster. (Overleaf) The finale of the International Dragon Boat Festival now held annually in Victoria harbour

Hong Kong is basically a city of immigrants. You get there, you try to make money there, and you get out; that has long been the city's overriding ethos. Hong Kong's tragedy is that it is full; it can no longer absorb masses of new people, be they escapees from dull and oppressive Chinese villages, or refugees from the Vietnamese Gulag. The bright lights still beckon, but rarely fulfil their promise: Vietnamese languish in camps, Chinese, when caught, which is often, are turned back across the border

The sea and it's ships surround Hong Kong. From busy sampans to
the stately junks, their great sails veined and shaped like moth's wings, to container ships
which bring Hong Kong's industry to the world. Hong Kong's deep water harbour,
a fine and sheltered anchorage, remains the lifeblood of the city

Times have changed and habits as well. Not too long ago no Chinese would have exposed themselves to the sun on a beach. Young girls would shade their pale faces behind a fan or beneath a parasol. Now however these inhibitions have gone. Western Coppertone and bronzed bodies reflect a youthful striving for health and body beautiful. Local beaches and colourful sailing regattas are now popular Chinese pastimes

A sky-ride in any of the 252 cable cars will bring you to "The Dragon"
at the Ocean Park, a roller coaster looping the air 400 feet above Deep Water Bay.
At 50 miles per hour it guarantees a thrill-of-a-life time ride,
but if your tastes lie elsewhere Hong Kong has natural parks of exotic birds,
a golden Pagoda housing over 100 species of gold fish—and the world's largest aquarium

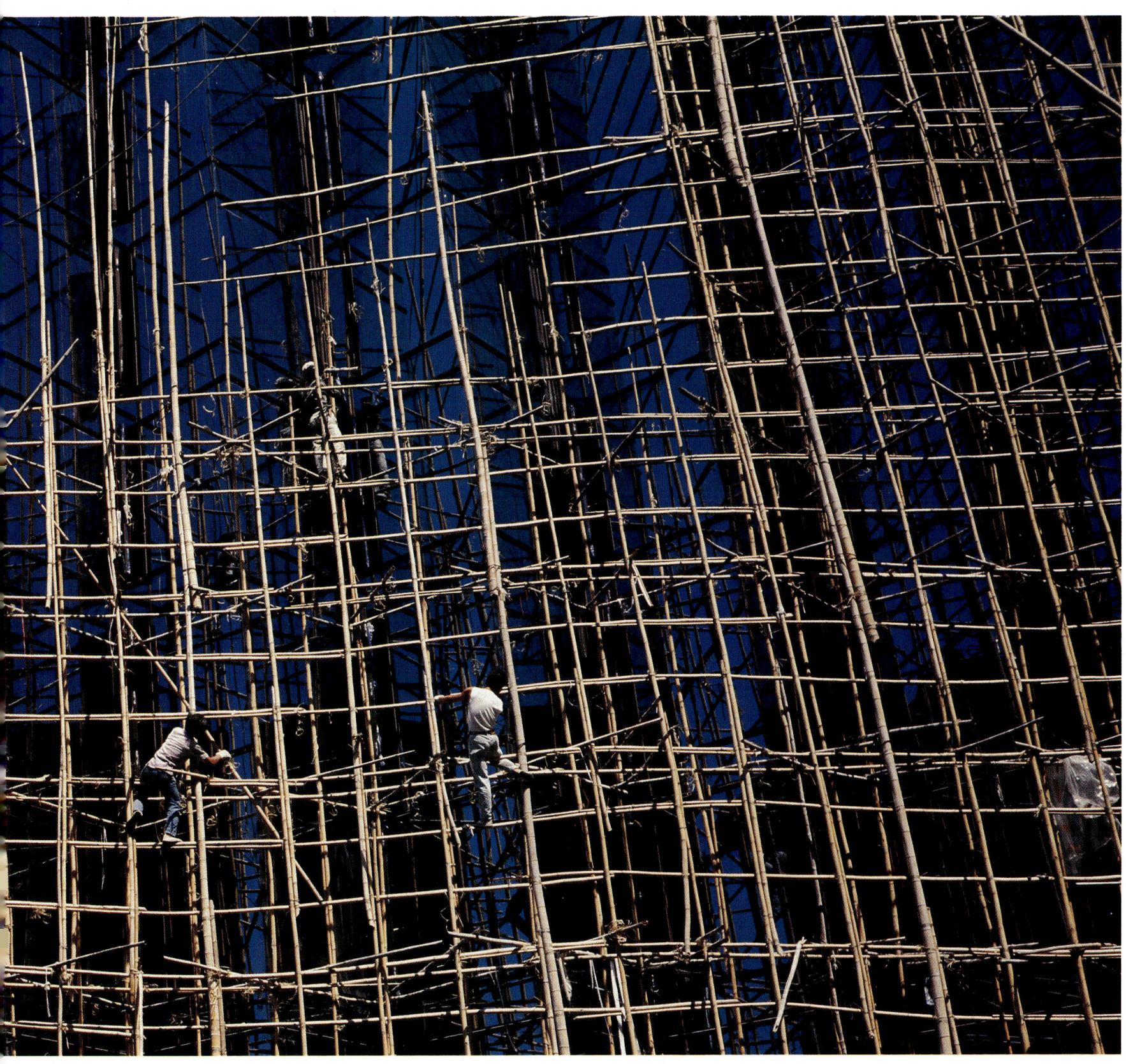

The clash of old and new appears in perpetual paradox. Behind the traditional bamboo screen lies some of the most spectacular modern architecture in the world. Here masters of this scaffolding craft remove the final bamboo poles to unveil the blue glass curtain wall of the recently opened Kowloon Hotel

As if trapped within a cage, a cowboy spurs his horse through the bamboo lattice work erected in front of a Texan-style advertisement. The art of bamboo scaffolding has a long tradition in Hong Kong. Lightweight and flexible, it is used extensively in the construction industry, even to the dizzy heights of 50-storey buildings. On more traditional lines, a Chinese opera house under construction uses bamboo exclusively for a village celebration

In Chinese opera, tradition is all. Every flowing movement, every splendid costume, every facial decoration has it's symbolic meaning, immediately apparent to those familiar with them. Cantonese opera often jerks more tears than the weepiest modern soap opera. Many of Hong Kong's older folk still love to agonize over the miseries suffered by young ladies at the hands of their mother-in-laws or heartless uncles

The Hong Kong year is colourfully punctuated by festivals and feast days, which embrace the entire population. The majority of festivals are observed according to the lunar calendar. Historically, Hong Kong people have always been dependent on the sea, first for fishing and later for trade. The most popular deities are those connected with the sea and the weather. Tin Hau, the Queen of Heaven and the protector of seafarers, is worshipped by a quarter of a million people

The manipulated smile of a wooden puppet-on-strings plays its role as spontaneously as the smile on the face of a punter at the races, despite the myth that Chinese are inscrutable

Horror expressed on his face an opera performer, who's civilization of tradition, ceremony, paint and clashing cymbals seems centuries removed from that of a youth orchestra musician pumping and blowing to coax a squeal from his bagpipes

Racing in Hong Kong mirrors the reckless entrepreneurial instinct of the territory. The invigorating uncertainties challenge the punters to chance their luck. Gambling is the spice of life for many Chinese. The winning horse, the lucky number, the right combination — must eventually come up trumps. In the heat of summer, races are suspended and horses are retained in air-conditioned stables at race tracks on either side of the harbour

Expatriates have their annual festival too: the Rugby Sevens Tournament, known for its fast football and the enormous consumption of beer. It has proven to be so successful that Australia made an attempt to kidnap the event and hold it Down Under

In the parks and green pathways every morning, Hong Kong people can be seen at
tai-chi practice which is as popular here as it is in China. The Chinese take proper breathing and graceful
movements very seriously. But traditional grace also finds more modern
expression on the rehearsal floors of mirrored studios throughout Hong Kong

Hong Kong is a young city. The people run in Marathons or on the spectacular
Eastern Island Corridor, specially closed off to traffic, they stroll on Sunday for a walk-for-a-million
charity, hoping to raise that sum of money for the community

The Dragon is the spirit of life and energy for the Chinese. His claws are in the forked
lightning and his scales glisten in typhoon storms as he leaps from winter darkness to renew the world.
Hong Kong auspiciously calls its northern hills Kowloon — Nine Dragons.
Colourful dragon dances are commonly performed at the commencement of new business.
Annually a Dragon Boat festival is held in the main harbour and parents arrange
births for the Dragon Year — most powerful in the Chinese Zodiac

Chinese learn their first lessons in life strapped to their mother's back. For this young girl the future is still a mystery as she peers questioningly out from the security and comfort of her mothers sling: For better or for worse Hong Kong still has the allure of sexual promise. Suzie Wongs offering mysterious and exoctic pleasures. Though reality is hardly mysterious and not always pleasurable. But Suzie Wongs don't come cheaply and their charms are an acquired taste

Those that dislike the crush of humans ought to stay away from Hong Kong. The place is awash with people, cheek by jowl, arm in arm, back to back, moving, ever forward, always in crowds. And yet, these crowds are not anonymous. The faces are never alike. What strikes one about Hong Kong crowds is the individuality of the people that form them and less the faceless tenemants they are housed in as seen at night on the following pages

The Governor of Hong Kong is the nearest thing the colony has to royalty.
The pomp and circumstance surrounding his activities are the last gasps of imperial glory.
They are rather splendid gasps, though, and as the end draws nearer, more than
a little poignant. The rituals of state can even be a moving experience, as was the funeral of
Sir Edward Youde, Hong Kong's 26th Governor. He was not the most flamboyant of governors,
but perhaps partly because of that surprisingly well loved, as was demonstrated by the large crowds
and city elders who came to pay their respects at his funeral in St. John's Cathedral (Overleaf)

The governor in his full regalia, the justices in their wigs, the cenotaph commemorating the Great War fought thousands of miles away in France, Turkey, in the mud of Flanders. These are symbols of another time, another place. They are no longer the marks of power, but the fast-fading afterglow of a bloody, glorious, venal, but all things considered, relatively decent history

Hong Kong's new governor, Sir David Wilson arriving at Edinburgh Place.
The Guard of Honour is formed by the 1st Battalion 2nd Kind Edward VII's own
Gurkha Rifles. The Gurkhas, now so much part of the Hong Kong landscape,
will go home after 1997. The governor's uniform, including the plumed
helmet and sword, will become a relic of the past. Sir David's main task
will be to ensure a smooth transition from British Raj to Chinese rule

A surreal kind of beauty can be found in unexpected places like the container port, which ranks among the top three of it's kind in the world, handling over 2.25 million containers per year. The container port west of the central harbour seen at dusk from Victoria Peak (Previous pages)

In Hong Kong new buildings appear to grow like rice after the rains. In the hazy distance the twin towers of the new Macau ferry pier await completion; in the foreground two workers scrub down a passenger ship alongside the Ocean Terminal

Despite the less than luxurious conditions, crammed into limited living conditions, Hong Kong people still retain their unique sense of humour and manage a giggle. On the left, Duty Free employees team-up to compete for the annual Dragon-Boat Festival. Hands which have generously contributed to life's toils lovingly caress an expressive face at one of many Helping Hand Charity homes in Hong Kong

Their laughs even seem to be quite scrutably genuine

Religion in Hong Kong, like everything else in the world's greatest Chinatown,
is a pragmatic affair. Families light joss sticks, worship gods, say their prayers,
not for some abstract spiritual purpose, but for direct gain, that is to say, for money,
perhaps the most worshipped god of all

Hong Kong relies heavily on the sea. Many of its people not only work on boats
but live on them too. Their hands are testimony to their tough lives,
and ever present are the gentle symbols of life's achievements, gold or jade.
Tin Hau is the goddess of seasoned seafarers and thus close to Hong Kong's heart.
First paper money is scattered on the water for the benefit of the sea spirits.
Then great sticks of incense are lit at the Tin Hau temple in Joss House Bay

Of the more than one thousand temples of Hong Kong, the Man Mo Temple, with it's destinctive coiled inscence burners, is perhaps the most well known if not the most impressive. Located in Hollywood Road in Central, near the great corporate and financial powerhouses of the colony, it offers an alternative way to aspire to riches. If luck in the stock market doesn't come through perhaps the gods in Hollywood Road might step in

Pockets of traditional Chinese temple architecture remain, especially outside the bustling city. These fierce-looking roof tiles stand guard over a temple at Fanling in the New Territories. Hong Kong has more than 360 Buddhist and Taoist temples, some centuries old and containing priceless antiques

As more and more young Chinese move away from their Hong Kong homes to bring more Chop Suey and Sweet and Sour Pork to the grateful outside world, the villages become increasingly empty. Without people, they die, slowly, with a residue of dignity lent by an ancient past

In the villages, too, materialism and spiritualism go hand in hand.
A fortune teller seeks mystical ways to promise people prosperity;
this elder makes a living from palm reading, choosing auspicious dates for marriages
and commencement of new businesses to writing a detailed life cycle chart
based on a person's birth sign and time and the *yin* and *yang*.
Trees are festooned with religious tokens, requests to the gods, paper money,
all serving one grand purpose. To aid that often elusive quest for riches

Along with the gods, the spirits of ancestors must be kept happy to ensure propriety
in this world. This means that food and other luxuries—
be it in the symbolic form of paper—are offered to ancestral spirits.
Once a year at the Spring Festival, graves are swept, food and drinks served.
And sometimes the ancestral bones are laid-out, cleaned and polished
before being consigned to an urn in the family shrine. The objects above
are not arcane religious symbols—but letter boxes in a New Territories village

On the islands and in the green New Territories the ancient rhythms of earth,
buffalo ploughing and growing things still create alliances and mutual interdependence.
Hong Kong is not often associated with the slow unchanging pleasures of rural life
but it exists nonetheless. The water buffaloes still serve man in the same way
they have done for thousands of years, by plowing rice paddies.
And even in Hong Kong the buffaloes can find an unhurried moment in
an odd muddy pool to rest and wallow in

The main form of recreation in Hong Kong is eating. Eating virtually anything.
As the northern Chinese like to say, a Cantonese will eat anything that walks,
floats or flies that is not made of steel. Ducks, for Peking duck,
no longer come from Peking. They are reared and prepared right here in the
New Territories of Hong Kong where farmers keep pace with supply and
demand for the territory's need of meat, fresh vegetables, eggs and poultry

Cultivating birds used to be an elegant pursuit of Chinese *literati*. Aged men love to take their precious songsters for strolls in their cages, ending up at the tea houses in old Shanghai Street or Queen's Road. Sipping tea among the homely debris of battered teapots and ancient spittoons, they will debate among themselves the merits of the warbler or the mavis and much prefer the high-pitched songs of their caged escorts to the tiresome chatter of humans

The greatest natural resource of Hong Kong are its people. It has always been a magnet, drawing to it those who sought a job, a home, or a park bench to dream of better things. When times in China turned troublesome, thousands of humbler labourers, coolies, fishermen, or rickshaw pullers would flock to Hong Kong and an unknown future. Today, few rickshaw pullers are left, as a concerted effort has been made to phase out this menial form of transport

Hong Kong people are early risers. At the first rays of the harsh morning sun, Chinese ladies will shade their faces behind a straw fan, for too much sun is deemed undesirable. A street sweeper with traditional hat, bamboo broom and basket brushes the curb to finish his early morning task ahead of the madding crowd

The virtue of age is respected in Chinese society. Especially with the regard of one who over the years has felt the golden glow of the sunrise over Hong Kong's harbour, as often as this lady has. Hong Kong possesses only one natural asset, a fine and sheltered anchorage — largely the reason for the British presence that began in 1840

In few of the great cities of the world is the future as uncertain and precarious as in Hong Kong. There is money in uncertainty, and the place thrives on speculation. So clearly the more you know about the future, the better, hence the enormous number of fortune tellers. To them, marriage, fortune and fame are no secrets

The written word is sacred to the Chinese. No wonder, then, that the art of writing Chinese characters, in stylised brush strokes, is regarded as one of the highest arts of all